TIME TO BE A TEEN

Your Power With Words

Claudine G. Wirths and
Mary Bowman-Kruhm
Cartoons by P. Stren

Twenty-First Century Books

A Division of Henry Holt and Company
New York

Twenty-First Century Books
A Division of Henry Holt and Company, Inc.
115 West 18th Street
New York, NY 10011

Henry Holt® and colophon are trademarks of
Henry Holt and Company, Inc.
Publishers since 1866

Text Copyright © 1993 by Claudine G. Wirths and Mary Bowman-Kruhm
Cartoons Copyright © 1993 by Patti Stren
All rights reserved.
Published in Canada by Fitzhenry & Whiteside Ltd.,
195 Allstate Parkway, Markham, Ontario L3R 4T8

Library of Congress Cataloging-in-Publication Data

Wirths, Claudine G.
   Your power with words / Claudine G. Wirths and Mary Bowman-Kruhm ;
Cartoons by Patti Stren.—1st ed.
     p. cm.—(Time to be a teen)
   Summary: Discusses in dialogue format how to use word power and
body langauge to improve communication skills.
    ISBN 0-8050-2075-6 (alk. paper)
   1. Interpersonal communication—Juvenile literature. 2. Nonverbal
communication—Juvenile literature. [1. Interpersonal relations.
2. Nonverbal communication.] I. Bowman-Kruhm, Mary. II. Stren,
Patti, ill. III. Title. IV. Series.
BF637.C45W578 1993
158'.2—dc20   93-4751
                                                                                                                                                          CIP
                                                                                                                                                          AC

First Edition—1993

Printed in the United States of America
All first editions are printed on acid-free paper ∞.

10 9 8 7 6 5 4 3 2 1

To Jenny and Becky McGonigle

Claudine G. Wirths and
Mary Bowman-Kruhm

This book is dedicated to the *most* dedicated researcher and archivist I've ever had the pleasure of working with . . . my mother.

P. Stren

Contents

Introduction Word Power	1
Chapter 1 Talk About It	3
Chapter 2 Face-to-Face	9
Chapter 3 Targeting Your Friends	19
Chapter 4 Targeting Your Teachers	26
Chapter 5 Speech! Speech!	33
Chapter 6 Targeting Other Adults	40
Chapter 7 What to Say When You Don't Know What to Say	47
Index	56

INTRODUCTION
Word Power

Do you ever:
- Try to tell your parents about something that happened at school, but they don't seem to hear?
- Start giving an oral report, but forget what to say next?
- Try to explain why your paper is late, but the teacher won't listen?
- Ask a store clerk to wait on you, and get yelled at for being rude?

1

Some kids never seem to have these problems. Teachers listen to them when they explain. Their parents ask them what's happening—and really tune in. Snippy store clerks willingly wait on them. Other kids want to hear what they have to say.

What do they know that most kids don't? They know the power of words and how to use that power.

In this book we'll show you how to use *word power*. We'll help you to know what to say and how to say it. We'll give you ideas that will help you to know when to talk and to whom to talk. We'll also tell you how to hear what others say to you. If you give our ideas a try, you may soon find that people start listening to you.

C.G.W.
M.B.-K.

1 Talk About It

Which of these four pairs of comments are you most likely to say when you are talking to someone?

You're lying!	or	That's not how I see it.
You're clumsy!	or	Let's try that again.
Go away!	or	When you do that, my head aches.
Shut up!	or	I need some time to think about this.

The ones on the left, but I guess that's wrong.

Surprise! Depending on the time, the place, and the person, any of the above might be a fine thing to say.

Since you "guess" you're wrong, you sound like a lot of teens we know. They tell us that they have a hard time knowing what to say when they talk to other people, especially adults. When they have something important to tell someone, they don't say what they mean to say or somehow their words come out all wrong.

That happens to me a lot.

It happens to all of us from time to time. But you can keep it from happening very often by knowing some tips and tricks of talking. We hope that by the time you finish this book, you'll have real *word power*. We think you'll find out how to say what you want to say.

This sounds like something I need. Is learning to talk with word power hard?

Not really. Word power is simply a matter of targeting your talking to others so that you will be listened to and understood.

That sounds as if I'm going to shoot at something!

Not that kind of target. We are saying that, before you open your mouth, you need to think about the person who will be listening to you. The more important the thing you have to say, the more you need to be sure the other person will listen to and understand you.

Word power can give you this confidence, and it can be summed up in three tips:

Tip 1. *When you say it* depends on when the other person is ready to hear you.

Tip 2. *What you say* has to be words that the other person can and will listen to and understand.

Tip 3. *How you say it* depends on your body language.

What do you mean in the first tip by choosing a time "when the other person is ready to hear you"?

If you really want the other person to listen, timing counts. Don't try to get your message across when:

- *The other person is thinking about or is doing something important.* Don't tell your dad you want an increase in your allowance when he is lying under the car, up to his elbows in grease.
- *The other person is angry, upset, or excited.* Don't ask your sister to be better about sharing after-dinner cleanup when she is getting ready for a date with a new boyfriend.
- *You are angry, upset, or excited.* When you are upset about a bad grade you got on a math test, don't talk to your best friend about giving back tapes borrowed a month ago.

If you say something at the wrong time, the person will, at best, pay no attention to you or will forget what you said. At worst, if you say something at the wrong time, you can land both of you in a *hot spot*.

What's a hot spot?

A hot spot is any time that you or the person to whom you are talking gets upset. The more upset one of you is, the more likely something will be said that will make matters worse. Hot spots can happen with anyone.

As soon as you realize you are in a hot spot because one of you is upset, stop talking. Relax by taking a deep breath or two. Then don't say anything until you have thought of some cool words to say. That brings us to Tip 2. Use words that the other person can and will listen to and will understand.

By cool words, do you mean saying something nice to the other person?

No, nor do we mean cool as in "alll riiiight!" We mean cool as in "turn down the heat." Cool words take away most of the dangers of a hot spot. Cool words:
- are not insulting (no swear words, dirty words, or name calling).
- are facts.
- are spoken in a quiet voice.

All the words in the right-hand column at the beginning of this chapter are cool words. The ones on the left are hot words. Hot words make people even more upset. When people get very upset, they barely hear what you are saying. They may think you said things that you didn't really say. Learn what your hot words are and never use them when you are trying to have an important talk with someone.

I thought you said it was okay to use the words on the left sometimes.

We were being tricky. If you have a best, best friend, you may have noticed that you can say almost anything to each other. In fact, one way people who are very close to each other show it is by calling each other names or by being insulting. You may use hot words, but you say them with a cool voice. It all depends on the tone of your voice when you say them, because even best friends can be hurt by hot words if they think for a moment that the words are really meant.

Never use those kinds of words with anyone else because they will not help and may both hurt the person who hears them and turn what is going on into a big deal, one that is hard to get out of easily.

Let's say someone has me all upset. There's no way I would think of those cool words when I'm really mad.

That's why you need to practice using some cool words before you get in a hot spot. But if you find that you are too upset to use cool words, tell the person you will talk later. Leave the room if you possibly can and get rid of your feelings in a safe way. Take a walk, hit a ball, or even punch a pillow. Just don't punch another person.

7

Wait until you are both calm before you talk again. Plan what your cool words will be. But get together before you have been upset with each other for so long that pride gets in the way of having a useful talk.

If you can't walk away from a hot spot, at least don't say anything more than you absolutely have to. Try to calm down, and don't let your face or body look angry.

Is that what you mean by the third tip?

Right. Tip 3 says, "How you say it depends on your body language."

Say some more about body language. I think I know what you mean, but I'm not sure.

Body language refers to all the body movements you make when you are trying to get your message across—how you sit or stand, what expression you have on your face, how you hold your hands, and so on. Body language is so important that we need to talk a lot more about it.

2 Face-to-Face

Introducing → The Official Body Language Quiz

(Just) Match Emotions to the Body above: HAPPY, I LIKE YOU, BORED, INTERESTED, STAY AWAY AND ...... SURPRISED!

Body language is a very powerful part of the way we talk. Our faces often tell more than our words and give power to what we say. That's why you need to read other people's body language as well as match your own body language to your words.

I never thought much about it before, but I wonder what I look like to others when I'm talking.

Learning how you sit, stand, and walk when you talk to other people is a very important part of getting word power. The best way to find out is to have someone take a video of you when you don't know you're being taped. Then you can see yourself the way others see you. If you don't know someone with a camcorder, check yourself in a mirror and also ask your best friend to tell you some of the things you do.

Don't forget to check for gestures such as chewing on your finger or twiddling a piece of hair. These actions tell other people that you are probably feeling nervous, anxious, or bored. Others also often find these gestures annoying. Here are some ways you might show how you feel by using some other common body language gestures:

angry	frowning, clenched fist, tight skin on jaw
happy	smiling, relaxed face, eyes open but relaxed
surprised	eyes wide open, lifted eyebrows
stand back	arms folded across chest
I like you	a light touch, standing close, smiling with mouth and eyes
hostile	pointing at someone with tense arm and hand, tense face
interested	leaning toward the other person
bored	leaning away from the other person, arms folded

I'm not sure I'll ever get up my nerve to say anything if I think all the time about how I look.

Not to worry. You'll find that using correct body language comes easily once you're aware of it. To know more about the fine points of body language, read some books on acting or sign up for a course in drama. Good acting is largely based on good body language, and acting can help you perfect your own body language.

To improve your understanding of body language, start paying attention to the body language of others. By watching members of your family, you'll soon learn that your family probably has some common body "words" that you all use. In one family we know, everyone in the family expresses pleasure at receiving a present by throwing their arms around the giver in a big hug. But in another family, the person who likes the present just looks up at the giver with a big smile and says thank you.

That sounds as though body language doesn't mean the same to everyone.

The answer to that is both yes and no. Most people in this country use similar gestures. However, people in other countries may have different ways of expressing their feelings, and within a family small signals develop that are unique to that family.

Husbands and wives often copy each other's body language, especially when they truly care for each other. The children often copy their parents' body language.

I know I can tell from just looking at my mom if she is in a good mood or not. I'm not sure how I know, but I do.

When you were a baby, you paid attention to her body language even before you could understand her words. By this age you know her so well that lots of times she doesn't have to say anything.

The next time you sense that she is in a good mood, look at her carefully and see if you can tell just how you know. Does she stand a certain way? Look at you straight on? Reach toward you? Then think about yourself. Do you do the same thing when you are in a good mood, or do you do something different from your mom?

Sometimes when I try to fool her, she says, "I can look at you and know you're not telling the truth." How can she do that?

The same way you know when she is in a good mood. Your body language can tell tales on you—especially if the truth doesn't match what you are saying. Your body language usually tells what you are really thinking. For example, most people show some tension in their faces when they lie. They may have tightness around the lips or may not look directly at the person to whom they are talking. They may talk too fast, or may stumble and stammer. So no matter what their words say, their body says they aren't telling the truth.

Are you saying that I can learn to lie to my mom if I learn how to act as if I'm not?

If our moms are any sample, the answer to that is no. Our moms can always tell if we are telling the truth. Moms seem to have a sixth sense when it comes to knowing when their kids are lying.

But my mom doesn't always seem to know when I need to talk to her. I tried to ask her something last night while she was fixing dinner, but she kept saying, "Ummm-mm." I don't think she was tuned in at all.

She was probably busy, and you didn't follow Tip 1 about picking your time. But in truth, even when you pick your time, you don't always get listened to by your folks the way you would like. Most of the time you can say just about anything, and they will both understand and be understanding because they know you so well. But sometimes getting parents to talk with you about something serious is very hard—especially now that you are changing from a little kid to a teen. They don't realize that you are growing up fast and need to talk about adult things.

That's true. On the other hand, sometimes when I want to know something, I can't get them to stop talking. Dad or Mom starts talking and gives me a big lecture! Why do parents do that? I ask a simple question

and want a simple answer. Twenty minutes later they're still going on and on.

When you ask them questions, they feel loved. They also feel as if they are being good parents when they give you lectures. You have grown up so fast, they fear that they haven't told you all you should know, so they try to take every chance to tell you more about everything.

What can I do to slow 'em down?

Ask your question by first saying, "I just need a short answer right now—no details." If your parent says, "But you need to know this, too," listen for a few sentences. Your parent may be right. However, if your eyes begin to glaze over, interrupt politely and say, "I need to go do . . . right now. Can we talk more later?"

If you have the time, listen to the whole lecture, even if it is one you've heard before. Not only will that make your parent feel good, you just might learn some stuff you need to know. Maybe not stuff you need to know right away, but later.

Well, how can I get them to stop and listen, really listen to me when I need to talk?

Here are suggestions that can help:
- Be sure you look fairly neat and tidy when you talk with them. Don't laugh at this suggestion. Parents and other adults will pay more attention to you if you are careful about how you look. That's a part of body language, too.

- Begin by asking if they have time to stop what they are doing for ten minutes and listen just to you.
- If they don't have the time then, ask them to name a time when they can. Then be sure to show up on time.
- When you do talk, remember to use cool words, and don't use teen slang that they don't understand.

But what do I say? Some things are hard to talk about.

Before you talk, plan what you are going to say. Ask yourself:

- "What is the exact problem, question, or complaint I want to talk about?"

    Example:
    My brother stays too long in the bathroom. I need more time first thing in the morning.

- "What are the facts I need to support my position?"

    Example:
    He took at least ten extra minutes three times this week so I had to rush to get ready for school. I talked to him, and he said he doesn't care.

- "What is the exact help or change I want?"

    Example:
    I want them to talk to my brother so I have my fair share of time in the bathroom and my brother will stick to the rules.

Can I add that he squeezed toothpaste into my mouthwash bottle?

Seems like a reasonable complaint to us—except that isn't the point you are trying to make. We bet that in this case, he is playing a joke on you! You must stick to the important facts about one thing when talking to your parents. Bringing up everything your brother ever did sounds as if you are just trying to sandbag him.

Why can't I just tell my brother to do what I want him to do?

That's harder, but not impossible. Although brothers and sisters can be your dearest friends, they can also make life a torment. When you need to say something serious to a brother or sister, use the three tips.

If your brother and sister are younger, you can talk with them most easily if you take them aside sometime and pay some special attention to them. Go to the mall and buy them a soda or take them for a walk down the street while you talk.

If your older brothers or sisters are real sports fans, don't try to talk to them when they're watching a ball game on TV. Talk to them as if they were grown-ups, and don't call them names or complain about everything they have ever done to you.

Pick one thing, and offer to make a deal to get what you want. For example, if bathroom time is a problem, suggest that both of you use a timer when you are in the bathroom. While you are there, the other person won't bug you and vice versa, but when the timer rings, each of you will leave promptly.

If making a deal doesn't work, take your problems to your folks and ask for a family meeting.

Our family gets together sometimes, but only if we're having a big problem.

A once-a-week meeting time is a good idea for every family. Ask your parents to set a time when family members can talk with one another. To be useful, a family meeting has to include everyone who lives under the same roof—a parent or parents, kids, grandparents, aunts, cousins, whoever.

Only a few rules for family meetings are needed. We suggest allowing each person to say what he or she wants to say for three minutes. No one interrupts or asks questions. Then each person in the room has two minutes to talk about what the speaker said or to ask questions. No name-calling or put-downs are allowed. And parents have the last word.

I'd really like that kind of meeting. My brother is always butting in when I try to tell my side of the story.

Don't forget that the rule will work two ways. When your brother talks for three minutes about the awful thing he thinks you did, you must sit there quietly and

17

say not one word until it is your turn to talk. Not being able to talk can be hard, but try a family conference. It may be better than the way you do it now.

3 Targeting Your Friends

If you are as lucky as many almost-teens, you have one or two special friends. You can say almost anything to them about whom you love, who annoys you, what scares you. They even know your middle name and don't tease you about it when anyone else is listening. Talking to them for hours is no problem.

Then there are other people you call friends who are not so close to you. When you are with them, you talk about fun things like other friends, school, music, teachers, parents, sports, and clubs. Sometimes talking to them can be a problem.

What can you say when you feel sort of shy? Even if you like to hang out with others, you don't always know what to say.

To start talking with people your own age or any other age, there are a couple of easy tricks that work.

- Ask the other person a question about some interest you might share. Don't ask anything too personal for starters. Start with something like, "Do you have any pets?" or "What's your favorite kind of music?" or "What do you think of so and so at school?"
- When the other person talks, look interested. Use your best body language: make eye contact, lean slightly forward.
- Be a good listener so that you can ask more questions about what the other person has said. If he or she wants to talk about country music and you don't know anything about it, ask what makes it special.
- Follow up with a statement of your own that is on the same topic.

What if the other person won't talk?

You can simply say, "Excuse me. I have to go check on something." Leave the room for a minute. When you come back in, talk to someone else.

I've got a special problem at school. I've started sitting at lunch with a bunch of kids who have been together for years. I don't know how to break into the conversation.

Try to get to the lunch table early for a few days and start talking to the first person to get there. When the others come, you will already be a part of the chatter.

But I can't get there early.

Then when you do get there, sit quietly for a while, but look interested as each person talks. When you do finally speak up, say something that lets the group know you have been paying attention. "Tony, you're right about our math teacher. I ran into the same problem with her last week."

But what about meeting a new group, like at camp? How do you start talking to people you don't know at all?

If the group is made up of both boys and girls, say something to one of the girls who is on the edge of the group. Girls are often more comfortable with a stranger talking to them than boys are. But boys or girls, just walk up to someone who is standing at the edge of the group and say hi. Tell them your name and find out theirs. Then follow the conversation tips.

Lately I've run into a problem. I'm getting to know some new kids at school, and when I bring them home, my mom gives them the third degree.

A good way to handle that is to tell your mom a little bit about your new friends before you bring them home. Moms like to know last names as well as first names. Write names down on a piece of paper if you have trouble remembering.

Let's say your new friend's name is Hank. When he gets to the house, say something like this: "Mom, this is Hank Smith. He's the friend I told you about who has just moved to our school. His dad has a job in town at that big office building."

Your mom may still ask a question or two, but then you say in a quiet voice, "Mom, we're in a hurry to listen to some tapes, so we want to get going. Okay?"

If Hank is smart, he'll tell your mom he's glad he met her. That lets her know he doesn't just see her as a piece of furniture. When you go to Hank's house, do the same. Be extra polite when you talk to his mom. Politeness always helps make you welcome.

One reason I like to go with friends to the fast-food place is that we don't have to worry about what we say. We can talk without adults listening in.

Hanging out with friends is a great way to get to know one another better. There's something about being part of a crowd that makes talk come easily. For that reason, keep in mind that other people are listening to you, and they will remember what you say.

Don't let talk at a time like this turn into making

fun of kids who aren't there. Putting down others seems to be catching. If you can think of some clever way to turn the talk to another topic, that's the best thing to do.

Be careful, too, of telling an idea or feeling you won't like to hear credited to you at school the next day. Save secret thoughts and feelings for only a very special friend.

I've noticed that boys at our school talk about different things than girls do. Is that true of other kids?

Generally, yes. People who study such things are not sure why, but from a very early age, most girls like to talk about feelings. Most boys like to talk about actions and ideas.

When a group of girls get together they say:

"Do you like her?"

"I wonder why my mom acts that way?"

"What can I do to get him to like me?"

"When we were playing field hockey, I felt like . . ."

Boys are interested in people, too, but they more often talk about their personal feelings only with a very, very close friend. With casual friends, they say:

"Guess what kind of car my dad bought!"

"Let's watch the ball game."

"I wish we could get tickets to their next concert."

"Do you want to trade me your Cal Ripken card?"

So if you want to make friends with someone of the opposite sex, keep in mind what that person likes to talk about and target what you say to his or her interests. But one thing we can tell you—boys or girls both say, "Pass the pizza!" You can always start a conversation by talking about food.

Now I've got a harder question for you. What can I say when a bunch of us are hanging out at the fast-food place and one of my friends really pushes me to do something that I don't want to do. Maybe it's wrong, or maybe I just don't want to do it.

When someone pressures you, the easiest (but hardest to say) answer is a simple no. But we can tell you some other things you might say. Pick one or two of the following sentences. Choose ones that feel right to you and best target the person who is pushing you. Practice in the mirror so that you are comfortable with saying what sounds right.

"Sorry, but I've got to go to . . ."

"My mom will ground me for a month if I do that. I'd miss . . ."

"I feel sick. You don't want me throwing up all over you, do you?"

"Not this time. I'm not in the mood."

"If you're really my friend, you wouldn't say that to me [ask me to do that]."

"I've got to make a phone call. Don't wait for me."

"I've got to go to the bathroom. Don't wait for me."

"I promised my dad I'd be home by . . . He and I are going to do a job together."

When you use one of these phrases, make sure your body language matches what you are saying. If you have said no to going to the mall afterward, put on your coat and head for the door; don't hang around as if you didn't mean what you said.

I think some of those phrases would work okay, but what do I say if I see someone is getting really mad at me for not going along with what he or she wants to do?

Remember, people who get mad when you won't go along with them are usually trying to make themselves feel okay about what they are doing. So don't rub it in that you think you are doing the right thing. Just repeat your statement in a calm voice. Don't try to answer questions or insults. Let your body language show your mind is made up and you are sure of what you said. Use word power.

4 Targeting Your Teachers

Most school staff—including teachers, administrators, librarians, nurses, and custodians—are people you don't know very well. You know their names and a few things about them, but not much else. The *you* they know is the you they see at school.

A few teachers may be closer friends. You visit their room before school, and you stop to talk with them at a ball game. In the classroom, however, they want you to act as if you are just another member of the class. What does this mean? This means that you have to learn to talk politely.

I don't want to run around sounding stuck-up.

We don't mean for you to say, "How *do* you *do*?" We are talking about three very simple things that will give you word power. When you speak politely:
- Look at the person. If you don't like to look the person in the eyes, look at a spot on his or her forehead just above the nose. You will look as though you are paying attention.
- Speak in a calm, quiet voice. Don't use slang or swear words.
- Stand or sit relaxed. By that we mean don't be moving around or fidgeting. If you are sitting, fold your hands in your lap. If you are standing, hold your hands either in front of you or behind you if you aren't comfortable just letting them hang down.

I guess I could do those things.

Always talk to every adult in a polite manner. As the conversation goes along, look for body language clues from the grown-up. If they keep standing or sitting stiffly and lean back from you or lean toward you in a way that makes you think they want to be in charge, continue to talk to them politely.

I try to be polite with adults, but I got nervous and tongue-tied the other day when the principal stopped me in the hall. All she said was, "How are you today?"

Principals do make lots of students nervous. Kids often think the principal is being sneaky and wants to catch them doing something wrong. Most of the time, school administrators are honest and up-front and simply want to get to know you or just be pleasant.

Next time, if you are between classes or have a pass, take what he or she says as being friendly. You can stop and say a few things about a ball game or your classes, if you have time. Remember to ask how he or she is. If you're in a hurry, say something like: "I have to run. I'm on an errand for . . . Have a nice day."

If you are in the hallway without a pass, quietly accept whatever you are told, head where you belong, and breathe a sigh of relief if you get off easily.

I often have trouble talking to some teachers in class. What can I say if I can't answer a question when the teacher calls on me?

Saying you don't know in a pleasant tone of voice is best if you don't know. If you need more time to think, here are some things to say:

- "Give me a minute to think about that."
- "I'm so busy listening that I need a minute to think."
- "I'm having a hard time following you. Can you say that in a different way?"
- "I don't know what you mean."

Sometimes scrunching down in the seat and trying not to get called on seems like the best way out.

That can work. But it's better to sit up and look interested. Teachers don't expect you to know everything, but they do like to feel you're part of the action. Just remember to use your polite voice in class.

But sometimes teachers make me so mad that it's hard to talk politely. My math teacher marked a problem wrong that I had right, and it gave me a lower grade. My brother said to forget it. I think I should argue with her about it.

Maybe not argue, but we think you should talk about it with the teacher.

So I go to the teacher's classroom . . . ?

Whoa! Before you see the teacher face-to-face, ask yourself: What will you say? How will you say it? When is a good time to see the teacher? Plan how to target the teacher, and prepare in front of a mirror first.

Do you mean talk to myself as if I'm talking to the teacher?

Yes, that's called *role-playing*. Role-playing, or acting out what may happen, is a great way to add to your word power by planning what you will say ahead of time. To role-play:

- Think first of a good way to begin, a simple state-

ment about why you are there and what you want.
- Then think about two or three things the teacher might say back to you.
- Think of an answer to each of those.

Here's how to make role-playing work for you.

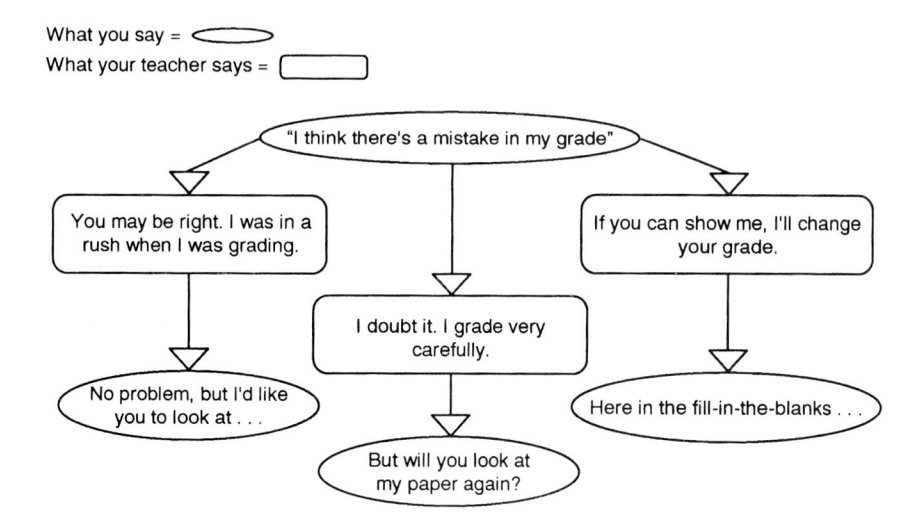

What you say = ⬭
What your teacher says = ▭

"I think there's a mistake in my grade"

You may be right. I was in a rush when I was grading.

I doubt it. I grade very carefully.

If you can show me, I'll change your grade.

No problem, but I'd like you to look at . . .

But will you look at my paper again?

Here in the fill-in-the-blanks . . .

Continue each of the ways your talk with the teacher might go. Practice them out loud. No matter what the result, end with a polite thank you to the teacher.

Role-playing on tape or in front of a friend can help, too. The meeting with your teacher may not happen just as you plan. But you will be a lot more ready to speak up about your problem than if you confront the person without any thought about what you will say or how you will say it.

One of my teachers called a boy in my class a real bad name the other day. What could he have done?

This is a hot spot. When a teacher does something wrong, you have to be very careful what you say and do. In the classroom the teacher is the law, but at the same time no teacher has the right to insult students or call them names. If it happens to you some time, the best thing to do is pretend you didn't hear. Teachers are human, too, and when they get tired or feel sick, they can say some stupid things.

However, if the teacher repeats the name-calling or makes a practice of it, you should talk to your parents. This is a time when adults need to talk to one another. Ask a parent to talk to the principal or meet with both principal and teacher. Give your parent the exact information about what was said, when, and why. In other words, help your mom or dad be ready to use cool words to solve the problem.

If I had a teacher who called me names, I'd never speak to that teacher again.

You may have to speak to that teacher. You don't have to be super friendly with anyone you don't like, not even a teacher, but you do need to be polite.

So what do I say?

Remember to use the three tips we gave you:
- Look at the person.

- Speak calmly.
- Be relaxed.

Those tips will give you the word power and confidence you need.

5 Speech! Speech!

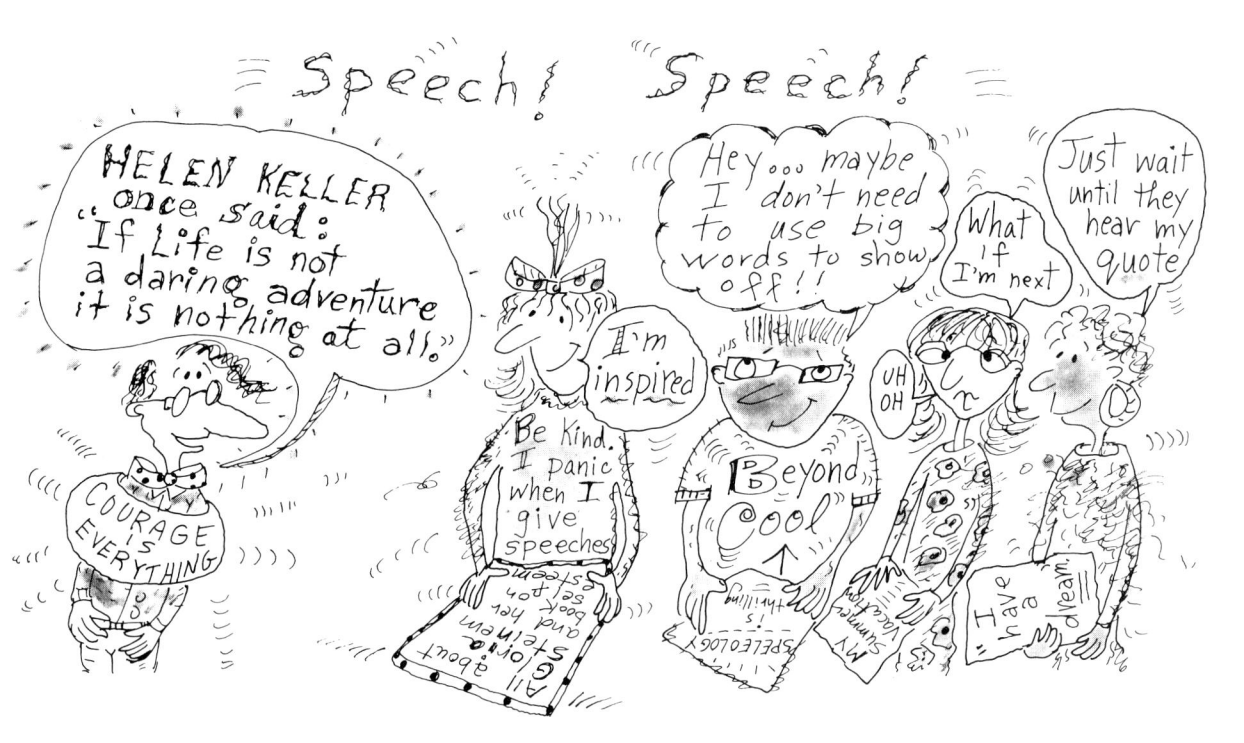

Many students tell us that giving a speech in class is one of the hardest things they have to do. How do you feel about it?

I hate it. I get really nervous.

Even actors and others who speak in front of lots of people for a living say they get nervous before they speak. A little feeling of nervousness is good; it can help you feel excited about what you're saying.

33

I have to give a speech next week. Maybe being a little nervous is good, but if I'm any more nervous, I'll throw up!

Feeling sure of yourself can do a lot to cure a shaky feeling. Practice at home, in front of your family. So that you can study how you will appear to an audience, ask someone to videotape you while you give the speech. A video will also allow you to see if your hands are waving around, if you are speaking to your shoes instead of the audience, and if note cards are in such clear view that people will look at them instead of you.

At the least, tape-record yourself. If you don't have a machine, ask to use one in the media center.

Even tape-recording won't help me remember what I want to say. Do you think note cards will help?

If your teacher allows them, note cards are helpful in reminding you of the major points you want to make. They also give you a nice, safe feeling. Jot down major points on cards and then, if needed, glance at them briefly.

Another way is to place a sheet of paper with an outline of your speech on a table or podium so that only you can see it. Memorize the first sentence exactly as you want to say it. Those few words will get you started.

Anything else I can do?

Body language also includes how you look. So to get

the most word power, dress neatly in clothes that you feel good wearing. Wear something near your face that will catch the eye of the audience, like a bright sweater, shirt, or scarf.

I've got a great pair of purple and red sunglasses I got on a trip last summer. That will make them look at me!

You don't want the kids laughing and the teacher angry. Just getting their attention is enough.

Should I memorize the whole speech?

Most people don't feel memorizing is a good idea. If you forget even one word, you may not be able to pick up and go on from there. It's better to practice a few times so you know what you want to say, but if you leave out a minor point, you won't be lost. You may also want to memorize a final sentence so you can sound strong at the end.

Maybe if I learn some big words to throw into my speech, I'll have real word power. All the teachers seem to think this girl who uses big words knows everything.

If using big words is not natural for you, memorizing some to toss out and impress is not a good idea. The girl may not know she uses them because, for her, they're natural.

On the other hand, simple words may have more

impact on people than fancy ones. Some speeches that are remembered for many years use easy words that everyone knows. Martin Luther King didn't say, "I possess in my mind a vision concerning the directionality of future events." He said, "I have a dream." The key is knowing when to use "big" words because they say just exactly what you mean and when to use everyday ones.

I guess I'd better stick to using words I know. What worries me most are my friends. What if they start giggling or making silly faces?

Think about what you're saying. Keep your mind on your speech to help you ignore anyone in the audience who is trying to upset you. Most of the time friends may tease you about upsetting your speech, but they like you too much to follow through and do it.

Suppose I make a mistake?

If you leave out a minor point, don't let on. Probably no one, including the teacher, will notice. If you leave out something important, admit it. Say, "I'm sorry, but I have to go back and tell you about . . . because it's important."

But what if I make a really big mistake? Last year a boy in our class was talking about model ship kits, and he got his words all mixed up. The other kids started laughing, so he did, too. Then the teacher thought he meant to say it, so she gave him a bad grade.

Everyone makes mistakes like that. We asked Jamie

Bragg, a long-time radio announcer on station WTOP in Washington, D.C., what he does when he goofs. Here's what he said: "I've said a couple of really bad things on the air. But I've learned to just keep right on talking like I never said it. If I don't laugh or stop and correct it, people will wonder if they really heard what they thought. After I leave the air, I can laugh about it."

I don't know if I can do that, but I'm glad to know that even guys like that have to watch what they say.

One more thing to watch is, pardon the pun, time. If you have to give a three-minute speech, you may think you know how long three minutes is—until you begin to speak. Practicing your speech will help you stay within the limit, but have some way to check your time while you're talking. If a clock isn't on a wall in front of you, put a watch where you can see it. Or ask a friend to give you a sign when your time is almost up.

There's a lot to remember! I'll sure be glad when this speech is over.

When you sit down, remind yourself of how nervous you were—and think about how nervous the next kid is. That person needs you to be a good listener, to help him or her get through their speech.

I'll try to be polite to help the other kids out. But why is listening a big deal? My English teacher even grades us on listening, and I think that's silly.

37

Listening is the flip side of talking. If you want to have real word power, talking is not enough. You must also hear what others say.

I've been listening since I was a baby.

True, but most of the listening you did when you were little was "easy listening."

Now that you are almost a teen, listening becomes harder for two reasons. First, you have conversations that are important and put you on the spot because you have to reply in the right way. Second, you are expected to listen for longer periods of time than when you were young.

After I listen for ten or maybe fifteen minutes, my mind takes off, and I think about something else.

Most people who have grown up with TV are used to listening for only that long. Then their mind breaks for a commercial. The most important thing to remember is: Your head has to be there. You have to focus on what the speaker is saying. Unless you pay attention to what's being said, you won't be able to understand it.

Can I do anything to help me pay attention longer?

You can do lots. Get enough sleep so you can focus at full brain power. Eat good meals; lots of candy and sweets at lunchtime can make you feel either very tired or very hyper—not feelings that help you focus.

Whether you're in class or out, paying attention is

easier if you join in. Ask questions or offer ideas. If talking out loud isn't a good idea, carry on a conversation in your head. "Did she say look at the picture on page 183? Check out the clothes those people are wearing. Oh, I see. Under the picture it explains . . ."

If you don't understand what someone (including the teacher) says, ask.

I wish I had thought of doing that the last time I talked to the doctor. I didn't understand half the words she used when she told me why I got sick.

Let's talk about some more of the problems you may have when you talk with adults.

6 Targeting Other Adults

Now that you are almost a teen, you are more and more on your own in an adult world, and many moments in life are spent talking with adults. That includes friends of your parents, parents of your friends, teachers, relatives, doctors, dentists and clerks at the stores where you shop.

It sure is an adult world. And dealing with adults isn't easy. I thought I was old enough to go to the doctor

40

alone. After all, she's been our family doctor since I was little. Then when I tried talking to her, my mind went blank. Afterward I couldn't remember what she told me to do for my cold.

Whenever you need to ask an adult for information, think ahead about what you need to know. For example, here are some questions to ask your doctor:
- What should I do to get better?
- When do I need to take my medicine?
- What caused this to happen, and can I do anything to keep it from happening again?
- When can I go back to school?

Answers to these questions won't cover every trip you make to a doctor's office, but they will take care of routine visits. Before you leave the office, repeat the answers, so you and the doctor are sure you understand. You may want to jot down what she says, show the notes to her, and ask if you have the information right.

While I was waiting in the doctor's office, this old lady tried to talk to me, but she was sort of deaf. I didn't know how to talk to her.

If a person seems to be hard of hearing, talk a little louder and a little slower—but don't shout. Don't turn away when you talk. Look the person in the eye so he or she can read your lips and your expression. That's a time to be sure you use body language.

But I started talking real slow and carefully to a man in a wheelchair who was at my dad's workplace, and he looked mad.

Just because people are in wheelchairs doesn't mean they are deaf or retarded. When in doubt, speak to a person who is handicapped as if he or she were normal in every way. If people look as through they might need some help, don't rush to help. Ask in a calm voice, "Do you need any help?" Then if they say yes, do what you can.

Talking about helping, a lady in the neighborhood asked my mom if I'd run an errand for her. I didn't mind helping this one time. When she gave me some money, I didn't want to take it, but I didn't know what to say.

You might have simply said, "No, thanks. I was glad to do it this time. I usually don't have time to run errands." Then you'd be off the hook if she asked you again. Or you might have said just thank you. She felt better about asking you to run the errand by giving you the money.

Saying thank you is really hard for me. It doesn't come out right.

The best way to say thank you is to look people in the eye and say a very direct thank you. If just "Thank you" sounds strange, try, "I really like what you did."

Saying "I'm sorry" is even harder than telling someone thanks.

No matter whether it is someone you know well or a stranger, the best way is to take a deep breath and say it—"I'm sorry for . . ." There is no easy way, but you'll feel a lot better after you do. Most adults will forgive you, and everything will be fine between you.

But sometimes adults don't say they're sorry! Last weekend I was standing quietly in a movie theater, waiting with my friend to buy popcorn. A man bumped my arm hard. I don't think he meant to, but I thought he might say he was sorry. Instead, he called me a name and muttered, "You kids think you own the world." I really felt like saying some hot words back to him.

Word power can make your life a lot easier when you interact with adults or other kids who don't treat you politely. Word power doesn't always mean saying something. It can also mean not saying anything.

But if I don't say anything, won't the other person think they're right, that I've backed down?

Yes, sometimes that will happen. But play out the event in your mind. What could happen if you don't back down? Today, too many people are all too willing to act dangerously when they are crossed.

Think about the problem in the movie theater. Is someone's crude and rude behavior worth your possibly getting thrown out of the theater or worse? Could you have changed the man's poor opinion of young people? Probably not in the few seconds you had with this stranger. Anything you said quickly and angrily would only confirm his opinion of teens.

Here are three rules to help you decide what, if anything, to say when you are in that kind of hot spot:
- *Think about the total picture* of what is happening.
- *Think through what you will do.* Try out the words and the actions that go with your words in your head before you speak. Don't let what the other person says suck you into saying or doing something for which you'll be sorry. These days you can't be too careful.
- *Talk cool.* Use cool words that will help calm the situation, not make matters worse. Also keep your body language cool. Don't make threatening or insulting gestures. Don't clinch your fist or laugh at the person. Simply turn away if you have to. You can always go to the movie another day.

The bottom line is: *Don't let pride or anger push you to say or do something foolish.*

I get really nervous at times like that.

You will do fine if you stay cool. Just be careful what you say. Here is a list of five things never to say to adults. These can only cause trouble:
- "Hey, you."
- "You can't make me."
- "I don't care."
- "Shut up!"

- Any swear words.

Are there five things that are *good* to say?

We'll give you our list. The first two, of course, are:
- "Please . . ."
- "Thank you." (No surprise here. Your mom probably told you the same thing.)

Here are three more things to say that will probably help a situation:
- "What do you think about . . . ?"
- "Can I help you?"
- "I have a problem. Can you help me?"

I don't understand that last one. How can asking for help give me word power?

Suppose on your birthday you get a tape that you already own. When you walk into a store to return it, you say, politely of course, "I want to return this tape, but I don't have a sales slip." How will the clerk answer?

With no sales slip the clerk will probably act as if I'm trying to rip the store off.

Now suppose you walk in and politely say, "I have a problem. Can you help me?" before you explain about the gift. Do you think your chance of making an exchange is better?

Probably a lot better. Knowing what to say and how to say it is hard. Mom tells me everyone in the family

45

clapped and was excited when I said my first word. If I had known what I was getting into, I might not have said anything after that.

There are many ways to say something. If you are sincere, most things you say will come out right. That's what word power is all about.

You said it!

7 What to Say When You Don't Know What to Say

What to say . . .

1. When you want to tell a boy or girl that you love them.

Stick to letting someone know why you care about them rather than saying you love them. You are less likely to get into more of a relationship than you want or to scare the other person away. The best way to let someone know you care is to pick out something specific about the other person that you think is special.

- "I really thought your speech in class was the best one."
- "I like the way you wear your clothes."
- "Nobody does as great cheers as you do."
- "What a race! You were super!"

2. When you want to break up with someone.

No matter what you say, the other person is likely to feel hurt, even if he or she wanted to break up, too, because that person feels rejected. Therefore, don't say anything until you are sure. But when you are sure, say clearly, "I'm sorry, but this isn't working out for me. I want to break up with you." Saying, "But we can still be friends," often makes the other person mad. Especially if he or she wants to be closer than that. Stick to a short, clear statement, and then don't let the other person's tears or anger or promises or threats get you to change.

3. When someone asks to copy your homework or look at your paper to cheat on a test.

The first time someone asks you for this kind of help, smile and say, "No way! You're on your own. Besides, I don't know how good mine is (or how much I know), and the teacher will catch on for sure if you make the same mistakes I do."

If someone keeps on asking you, say something like this: "I don't want to take a chance of you or me getting caught cheating. Please don't ask me again."

If the person keeps on, go to a counselor. The other

person needs some help—probably more help than you can give. If the other person threatens you, go at once to a counselor or the principal. Go the first time you are threatened.

4. When you want to tell a girl or boy that nobody likes to be around them because she/he smells bad.

If you tell the person, he or she may not know how to change, and all you will do is make the girl or boy mad. Instead, go to the school nurse or to a counselor or to some teacher that all the kids like. Say, "Can you help . . . ? She (he) smells bad a lot of the time, and it keeps her (him) from making friends. Please don't say I told you." Most counselors or teachers or nurses will take it from there. Don't make fun of this person; they may have a health problem.

5. When someone is driving you nuts because he or she is a loudmouth or uses swear words all the time.

Try telling the person directly. Say something like, "I like you, but when you talk so loud and make so much noise, I feel like taking off and going someplace else." Or, "Enough with the swear words! We know what you mean without all that garbage mouth stuff!" Say this with a smile and make sure the person knows you aren't mad.

6. When you see a boy's girlfriend holding hands with another guy (or the other way around).

Mind your own business. He'll find out for himself

soon enough. He'll probably not believe you if you tell, and he may turn against you instead of against the girl. (Same advice, no matter if the one being untrue is a boy.)

7. When a friend (?) has been telling bad things about you behind your back.

Tell this friend what you have been hearing. Tell the person that if he or she still want to be friends, cut it out now. It isn't always easy to talk about bad feelings, but sometimes you have to. If the person gets mad or won't deal with you about the problem, then you know he or she really wasn't much of a friend.

8. When you want to get into the super in-group in your school.

Sorry, but there's nothing you can say that will guarantee that you will be admitted. Close groups like that are often closed groups. Best advice is to be pleasant to the members, say hello and act friendly, but forget trying to get into the circle.

Look around for other people like yourself. Start with one person who likes the things you like, and soon you will have your own group—even if there are only two or three of you. Don't waste your time and breath trying to talk your way into any group that doesn't want you.

9. When someone is very sick or is in the hospital.

Try these tips:

- When you enter the room say, "Hi! I'm here to cheer

you up!" or something similar. Don't ask now for details about how the person is doing. If they want you to know, they'll tell you.

- Talk about the things you've always talked about. If you think either of you may be shy about talking, bring along a game or puzzle or magazine to share and to talk about.
- Don't talk about other sick people or people who have had horrible times with the same sickness. People who are sick don't want to hear it.
- Don't stay too long. People who are sick get tired more easily, and talk can be tiring. Before going in, ask someone in charge how long you should stay, and stick to it, even if your friend asks you to stay longer. Tell them you'll come back another time.
- When you leave, say good-bye, and if they are special in your life, tell them that you like them or really miss them when they aren't around.

10. When you are at a wedding, family reunion, funeral, or other adult occasion.

What you say doesn't have to be original, just polite, since these are mostly relatives. Say you enjoyed the wedding and are glad they invited you. At a funeral simply say, "I'm very sorry." Trying to be original or clever in any stressful situation usually blows up in your face.

Remember that adults often don't know what to say

either, especially to a young person they seldom see and with whom they don't have a lot in common. Think of some things ahead of time that you can ask them. Or have a few things in mind to tell them like, "I'm playing on a softball team. It's been a lot of fun."

11. When you promised a friend you wouldn't tell, but you are afraid the friend is getting involved with alcohol or drugs.

If you truly believe that your friend has tried one, and only one, time, keep the secret. But if you think alcohol or drug use has begun to be often, warn your friend to cut it out or you will tell someone. Offer to help your friend find the right person who will know how to help the person stop. When friends have serious problems, the best way you can help is to tell an adult who knows what to do. Go to a school counselor or nurse and say you have reason to believe that so-and-so is into alcohol or drugs. Ask the counselor not to use your name, but ask them to help that person.

If your friend finds out that you told someone, say you did it because he or she is a special friend. The person may still be angry and pull away from you, but you will have been honest if you say you truly care.

12. When you answer the phone.

Whoever answers the phone represents the whole family to the person at the other end. That's why you need to answer in an adult way. The best idea is to agree as a family on how the phone should be answered. Remember, the person on the other end can't see you—your body language doesn't help that person to know what you are saying. This makes it harder for the caller to understand directions or your feelings. You have to choose your words even more carefully than usual.

13. When you are supposed to say something after an adult tells you a story about his or her childhood.

Say something polite like, "That is something!" You can say that in a different tone of voice for lots of different situations. Don't ever say, "You told me that story before." Just listen politely and excuse yourself before the next story.

About the Authors

Claudine G. Wirths has a master's degree in psychology and another in special education. She has been a police psychologist and consultant in environmental decision making as well as an educator and member of the adjunct faculty of Frederick (Maryland) Community College. She is now a full-time consultant, speaker, and freelance writer.

Mary Bowman-Kruhm has a doctorate in education. She was a teacher and administrator with Montgomery County (Maryland) Public Schools in regular and special education and has taught at the University of Maryland and Western Maryland College. She is now a full-time freelance writer and consultant/speaker.

Other books by this writing team include *I Hate School! How to Hang In & When to Drop Out* (Harper & Row, 1987), *Where's My Other Sock? How to Get Organized and Drive Your Parents and Teachers Crazy* (Harper & Row, 1989), and *Are You My Type? Or Why Aren't You More Like Me?* (Consulting Psychologists Press, Inc., 1992).

The authors are pleased to be reunited with the illustrator of *I Hate School* on this new project.

Introducing P. Stren

P. Stren has written and illustrated sixteen books including **I WAS A 15-YEAR-OLD BLIMP, I HATE SCHOOL, FOR SALE: ONE BROTHER** and **HUG ME**. She has created <u>The World of P. Stren</u> and <u>Parlez-Vous Francais?</u>, rubber stamp lines for Rubber Stamps of America. You can find these amazing stamps incorporated into her most recent books.

You can also find her quirky cartoons in her most recent books. Some of her latest cartoons were used by designer Nicole Miller on ties and scarves. (P. Stren admits that she simply *lives* to do cartoons!)

P. Stren is a Canadian. She began her art career in Canada but eventually made her way to New York City where she took the School of Visual Arts by storm! She loved New York so much that she still lives there with her husband, a physician, and their menagerie: a sheltie, an orphan dog from Mexico and a python named Bubba.

55

INDEX

Acting, 11
Acting out (role-playing), 29–30
Adults, 39–45. *See also* Parents; Teachers.
   anger at, 31–32, 43–45
   apologizing to, 42–43
   childhood stories of, 53
   deaf, 41
   saying "no thank you" to, 42
   saying "thank you" to, 45
   at social occasions, 51–52
Alcohol or drug problems, 52

Body language, 8–14
   adults and, 11–12, 14, 27
   cool, 44
   deaf people and, 41
   friends and, 20, 25
   lying and, 12–13
   speeches and, 34–35
Body odor, telling someone about, 49
Boyfriends, 47–50
Boys, talking to, 23–24
Bragg, Jamie, 36–37
Brothers and sisters, 15–18

Cheating, 48–49
Cool voice, 7
Cool words, 6–8, 15, 44
Counselors, asking help from, 48–49

Deaf people, 41
Doctors, 39–41
Drama courses, 11
Drug problems, friends and, 52

Facial expressions, 10
Family, body language of, 11–12
Family meetings, 17–18
Family reunions, 51–52
Friends, 7, 19–26
   making, 20–22
   pressure from, 24–25
   saying bad things about you behind your back and, 50
   teachers as, 26
Funerals, 51–52

Gestures, 10, 34
Girlfriends, 47–50
Girls, talking to, 23–24

Groups, 21–23, 50

Handicapped people, 42
Help, asking for, 45, 48–49
Homework, copying, 48
Hospital, visiting people in, 50–51
Hot spots, 6–8, 31, 43–44
Hot words, 6–7, 43

Lecture, from parents, 13–14
Listening, 20, 37–39
Loudmouths, 49
Lying, 12–13

Mother, 12–13

Parents, 11–18
   family meeting and, 17–18
   friends and, 21–22
   lecture from, 13–14
   Politeness, adults and, 27, 43–44, 51–53
   teachers and, 27, 31–32
Pride, 44
Principal, 27–28
Problems, 45, 48–49, 52

Role-playing, 29–30

School, 26–32
School nurse, 49
Shyness, 20
Sick people, 50–51

Sisters. *See* Brothers and sisters.
Slang, parents and, 15
Social occasions, adults at, 51–52
Speeches, 33–37
   mistakes in, 36
   nervousness before, 33–34
   tape-recording yourself, 34
   timing, 37
   videotaping yourself, 34
Swear words, 49

Targeting, 4, 29–30
Teachers, 26–32
   being called on by, 28–29
   body language and, 27
   as friends, 26
   hot spots and, 31
   name calling by, 31
   politeness and, 27, 31–32
   role-playing and, 29–30
   targeting, 29–30
Telephone, answering, 52–53
Tests, cheating on, 48–49
Timing, 5–8
   hot spots and, 6–8
   parents and, 13–15, 17
   of speeches, 37
Tone of voice, 7

Voice, 7

Weddings, 51–52